Victorian railways

Fiona Reynoldson

This book is about the early days of rail and steam transport. It tells about the people who designed and built the railways, and about travelling by steam train in Victorian times.

If you are using the book to find out particular facts about Victorian railways, you do not have to read it all. Look at the **contents** (below) or the **index** (at the back) to find the best pages to help you. Then just read as much as you need to read.

The basic facts are given in big print, and more detailed information is in smaller print.

Contents

1 Introduction

The strength of steam

Steam was important in Victorian times because it was a new power that was used to drive machines.

Steam can be very powerful. It can make things move. When water is heated to boiling point it turns to steam. Steam takes up more room than water so steam can push the lid off a saucepan.

Just as steam can push the lid off a saucepan, it can also push other things. If there is enough steam it can push a train along a railway track.

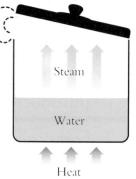

A steam train coming out of a tunnel.

Travel before steam

In Victorian times, people travelled in stagecoaches pulled by four horses. The passengers sat on top of the stagecoach or if they paid more money they could sit inside. The coach travelled at about 12 kilometres per hour.

Rich people had their own carriages and if they had the very best horses they could travel at about 24 kilometres per hour for short distances. Poor people could not afford to go by coach so they usually walked everywhere.

2 Early railways

A railway is made of iron rails laid on the ground. The wheels of the train run along the rails. In the early days horses pulled trains but very soon horses were replaced by steam locomotives which went much faster.

Railway trucks pulled by horses.

Iron railway lines are held in place by wooden planks called sleepers. Steam locomotives were much heavier than horses so it was important that the railway lines were built on firm ground.

The ground had to be as level as possible because the very first locomotives could not pull trains up even the smallest hills. These early steam engines were quite dangerous. Sometimes they fell off the rails and sometimes they blew up.

One of the earliest steam locomotives.

Chat Moss

At first, railway builders used wooden rails but they soon found that iron was stronger and lasted longer. Wooden sleepers held the rails the right distance apart and they also stopped the rails from moving when a heavy locomotive and train ran along them.

The railway track had to be on a firm base. George Stephenson wanted to build a railway across a bog called Chat Moss. Everyone said it was impossible because even a man walking on the bog sank right in but Stephenson was able to solve the problem. He ordered cartload after cartload of rubble and bricks.

These were poured into the bog until there was a high embankment. Then Stephenson laid the iron railway on top of that embankment. The railway ran straight and level across Chat Moss to Liverpool.

The railway on Chat Moss.

3 Keeping railways level

The first steam locomotives could not pull trains up hills so railway builders had to make the ground flat. They did this by cutting through hills and by bridging valleys.

This viaduct was built as the only way to cross the valley.

To keep the railway track as flat as possible the builders
dug tunnels under the hills and viaducts across the valleys.

Tunnels were blasted through rock or dug through earth.
Viaducts were built of stone, iron or wood across valleys so
that the trains did not have to go down one side of the
valley and up the other.

⬆ A railway viaduct carrying trains over a city.

↑ It took a long time to build a railway tunnel.

Box Tunnel

Box Tunnel is a famous example of a tunnel. It was built on the Great Western Railway near the city of Bath. The tunnel was three kilometres long and went right through the hill.

One gang of workers started digging at one side of the hill. The other gang started on the other side. For most of the way, the earth was clay, which is very soft and so the tunnel had to be lined with bricks. The men and horses worked deep under the hill with only candles for light.

The men dug and blasted away the earth and rock for over two years. They used one tonne of gunpowder and one tonne of candles every week.

Slowly the two gangs of workers dug towards each other. Even Isambard Kingdom Brunel, who designed the tunnel, was not certain that the two gangs were going to meet in the middle. Finally a hole was knocked through between the two ends of the tunnel. A great cheer went up from all the men. Brunel was so pleased that he took a signet ring from his finger and gave it to the foreman who was in charge of the two gangs.

4 First steam locomotives

A steam locomotive is a steam engine that moves on wheels. The boiler heats up water to make steam and the steam pushes the pistons which push the wheels round.

Richard Trevithick was the first person to put a steam engine on wheels in 1803. This was the first steam locomotive. Soon other people built steam locomotives to run on the new railway lines that were being built all over Britain.

Richard Trevithick.

The *Catch-me-who-can* engine, built by Richard Trevithick.

The opening ceremony of the Stockton to Darlington railway lines.

After Richard Trevithick had made the first steam locomotive several other engineers, including George Stephenson, built locomotives to pull trucks at coal-mines. Then, in 1825, Stephenson was asked to build a railway line between Stockton and Darlington for a wealthy business man.

Stephenson built a locomotive called *Locomotion*. It ran on the new track for a month before it blew up.

5 Steam engines or steam locomotives?

Many people felt it would be safer to have horses rather than engines to pull trucks on the railways. However, Stephenson and other engineers kept on making new locomotives.

Some businessmen wanted a railway between Liverpool and Manchester so they asked Stephenson to build the line. The businessmen ran a competition to find the best locomotive to pull the trains.

George Stephenson and his family.

Some people suggested that it would be safer to pull trains using a stationary steam engine. The engine was put in a shed beside the railway and chains were tied to the train. The steam engine puffed away and wound the chains, pulling the train along the track.

Stephenson thought it was much better to build a moving engine on wheels. So, when the Liverpool and Manchester railway was finished, a competition was held to find the best and safest steam locomotive. The competition was called the Rainhill Trials. Stephenson won the competition with his new locomotive called the *Rocket*.

The *Rocket* winning the Rainhill Trials.

First and third class carriages.

The Rainhill Trials

Five locomotives entered the Rainhill Trials. One was powered by horses but it was too slow. Another locomotive arrived too late to take part in the competition so that left only three locomotives.

The three locomotives were called the *Novelty*, the *Sanspareil* and the *Rocket*. The *Novelty* was fast and pulled a heavy train. It reached a speed of 34 km/h pulling 45 people but a boiler pipe burst so it was considered unreliable.

The *Sanspareil* was built by Timothy Hackworth and it looked good but it was very heavy and used a lot of coal. During the competition, a crack appeared in one cylinder and the locomotive broke down. Hackworth was very angry that the cylinder had cracked. He blamed Stephenson who had made the cylinder for him and he was even more angry when Stephenson's own locomotive, the *Rocket*, won.

The *Rocket* was a very good locomotive mainly because it was very reliable. It pulled a train at a steady 25 km/h for 110 kilometres without any problems. Its top speed was 47 km/h. Stephenson was delighted when he won and he was asked to build seven more locomotives to pull trains for passengers and goods for the Liverpool and Manchester line.

6 Travelling by train

Soon railway lines were being built all over Britain. Passengers travelled in first, second or third class carriages behind smoking, puffing steam locomotives.

By mid-Victorian times, parcels and letters were sent by train. Milk was sent to towns by train and ordinary people started to travel to work by train.
Many people went on holiday by train.
Even Queen Victoria decided to travel this way.
She ordered her own carriages to be made.

This carriage was used by Queen Victoria.

↑ Inside a third class railway carriage.

By the 1850s, trains were beginning to change the life of many people in Britain. Lots of people travelled by train. Passengers paid different fares to travel first, second or third class. First class carriages had padded seats but, in the early days, third class passengers travelled in open trucks and had no seats.

Trains brought fresh fruit, milk and vegetables from the country to the towns and the Post Office gave up using stagecoaches and sent all the mail by train.

People could live in the country and catch a train to work in the town. They could also afford to go on holiday by train to places like Blackpool or Brighton.

The Great Exhibition

In 1851, lots of people travelled on trains for the first time. They went to the Great Exhibition in London. This exhibition showed all the wonderful new inventions and machines that were being made. It was so popular that it stayed open for 140 days and was visited by six million people. Many of them arrived by train.

A man called Thomas Cook decided that he could make some money by organising excursion trains. In this way people from as far away as York could visit the Great Exhibition. The return Third Class fare was only five shillings.

Unfortunately for Thomas Cook, other people had the same idea about running excursion trains. Soon several railway companies were offering cheap fares to London. Thomas Cook had to cut his prices and in the end he did not make any money on taking 140,000 people to see the Great Exhibition. The excursions made him famous and he founded the first travel agents firm.

A ticket for the train to the Great Exhibition.

A poster advertising Thomas Cook's Excursions. ➡➡

The Great Exhibition was held in the Crystal Palace.

17

7 The stations

Railway stations were the places where the trains stopped so that the passengers could get on or off the trains.

The first railway stations were inns beside the railway lines. Later, proper stations were built. Different railway companies owned different railways, including all the lines and the stations.

▲ A country railway station.

When the railway lines were finished, railway stations were built beside the lines. At first, stations were inns where passengers could buy food as well as their tickets. There were no raised platforms so it was very easy to walk on to the track and there were a lot of accidents.

The railways became so popular that it was not long before special stations were built. The big city stations had many platforms but the country stations were small.

Often the trains only stopped at a small station if the station master put a lighted candle in the window to show that a passenger wanted to catch the train. Some railway companies provided a better service than others.

A city railway station.

Swindon Station

When the London to Bristol line was first completed there was only one station. This was at Swindon. A famous engineer, called Brunel, designed the station. A hotel and dining room were added to it.

Neither Brunel, nor the Great Western Railway Company who owned the line, wanted to run the hotel or dining room so they signed an agreement with a man called Mr. Griffiths. Mr. Griffiths paid the railway company one penny a year for the right to be the only person selling refreshments on the railway. In return, the railway company agreed that all the trains had to stop at Swindon for at least ten minutes.

Mr. Griffiths made a fortune. By the time passengers reached Swindon they were thirsty and hungry. They poured off the train into the dining room where Mr. Griffiths charged them sixpence (about £1.00 today) for a cup of tea. He also sold them expensive pork pies which he made himself from the pigs he kept in the station yard.

The passengers were always complaining to the railway company about the expensive food and drinks. Brunel himself complained about the coffee.

Here is a letter from Brunel to Mr. Griffiths:

Dear Sir,

I assure you Mr Player was wrong in supposing that I thought you purchased bad coffee. I thought I said I was surprised you should buy such bad roasted corn. I did not believe you had such a thing as coffee in the place. I am certain I never tasted any. I have long ceased to make complaints at Swindon. I avoid taking anything there when I can help it.

Yours faithfully,
I.K. Brunel.

Swindon. All the buildings near the railway line were to do with the railway.

8 Railway signals

There were lots of accidents in the early years of steam trains. The first trains often broke down and there were no signals. The early trains did not even have brakes.

However, engineers soon managed to fit brakes and they invented signals to control the number of trains travelling on a line.

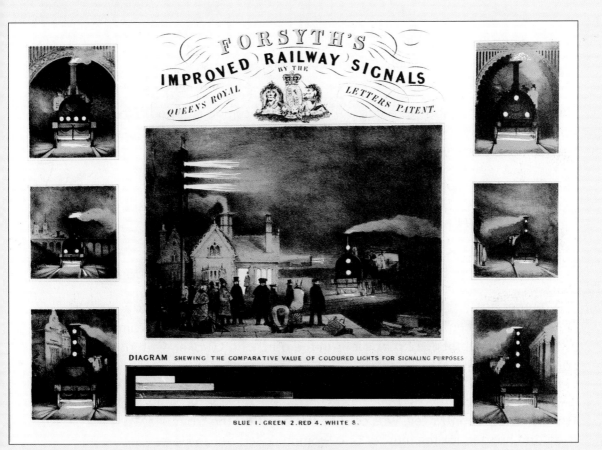

The first signals were operated by a man standing by the track.

The first railway signals were flags. A railway policeman stopped a train by standing at the side of the track with a flag. He allowed ten minutes between one train and another.

The electric telegraph was first used as a sort of signal in 1837. It was used to send messages to stations down the line and it was later used to regulate the number of trains on the line.

One message sent by the new electric telegraph in 1845 became famous:

"A murder has just been committed at Salthill, and the suspected murderer was seen to take a First Class ticket for London by the train which left Slough at 7.42 p.m. He is in the garb of a Quaker, with a brown greatcoat on."

The murderer, John Tawell, was caught as he got off the train. He was tried and hanged for the murder of a woman called Sarah Hart.

9 The life of a railway engineer

Engineers make machines. The railways were built by engineers who designed everything from the rail track and the bridges to the tunnels and the steam locomotives.

Two famous railway engineers were George Stephenson and Isambard Kingdom Brunel.

Isambard Kingdom Brunel is standing in the front row, second from right.

Bridges for railways had to be built across rivers.

The great railway engineers liked to have a hand in every part of building the railway. George Stephenson built the first successful steam locomotive called the *Rocket*. He built the first public railway line between Liverpool and Manchester in 1830. He was helped by his son Robert, who was a good engineer too. He went on to build steam locomotives and some famous bridges.

Although Isambard Kingdom Brunel was a rival of the Stephensons, he was also a great friend of Robert's. Here is part of a letter from Brunel to Robert Stephenson in 1840:

"My Dear Stephenson – We have given out that we shall open our line 30 miles further by 1 May. Our line will be ready but we shall be short of steam power. Another locomotive would make us easy. Now can you by any extra effort deliver us one in March?"

24

Isambard Kingdom Brunel (1806-1859)

Brunel was the son of an engineer. He started work by helping his father to build a tunnel under the River Thames in London. Then came a chance to build one of the new railway lines. In 1833, the directors of the Great Western Railway Company asked Brunel to be their engineer. Brunel was fascinated by the new railways. He had seen how successful George Stephenson's Liverpool to Manchester railway was and now he had a chance to build his own railway.

Brunel designed everything on the line from the tunnels to the signals. Unlike Stephenson, he decided that the railway lines should be very wide apart. He said this would make the trains steadier on the tracks.

The one thing that Brunel did not design was the steam locomotive but even then he made lots of suggestions for how it should be made.

This is one of the earliest photographs of a steam locomotive.

10 The life of a navvy

Navvies were the men who built the railways. They dug out the earth and laid the railway lines. Many navvies worked together in gangs to build the lines and they lived in huts close to the railway. They wore moleskin trousers and coloured waistcoats and they were often paid twice as much as ordinary labourers.

Railway navvies taking a break.

Blasting rocks to make a cutting.

Sometimes as many as 2000 men worked on a railway line. They worked in all weathers. In winter they worked up to their knees in mud while in summer they worked through the dust and the heat.

All the work was done with picks and shovels and wheelbarrows. Sometimes the navvies were helped by horses who pulled trucks and barrows for them.

Gunpowder was used to blast away rock. This was dangerous and uncomfortable. Many navvies were injured when the gunpowder blew out the rock and some were killed.

▲ Digging a cutting.

The boy who ran away

A navvy wrote about his life in a magazine called *Household Words*. We do not know his name but he wrote vividly about the life he led building the railways and living in the shanty towns beside the tracks.

He ran away from home when he was a boy and walked nearly 50 kilometres to the nearest railway works and asked for a job. He was taken on as a tip-driver which meant he had to drive a horse and cart full of earth dug up by the navvies.

When he was older, he became a navvy himself and earned good money working in a gang of about 40 men. His workmates all had nicknames. There was Happy Jack, Billygoat, Redhead, Fryingpan and many others.

Fifteen of them lived in a large hut with bunks at one end. Near the window were benches where the navvies played cards or ate their meals. The hut was a crowded place.

They employed a woman to cook for them called Old Peg. She kept the keys to the beer barrels but could not stop the men from getting drunk and fighting.

Old Peg did rule over the kitchen where she had pots and pans and a locker for each man's food. She cooked in a huge cauldron over a blazing fire. In the cauldron, each man's food hung in a bag, on a separate piece of string, in the boiling water.

11 Summary

Steam transport changed the way people lived. In 1825 there were 14 kilometres of railways in Britain but by 1900 there were 29,000 kilometres and there were railways all over Europe, America and elsewhere too. Instead of travelling at about 15 kilometres an hour, people could travel at 100 kilometres or more an hour. They could go further and faster.

Engineers like Trevithick and Stephenson built big, powerful steam locomotives that could pull trains loaded with people or goods all over Britain. Together with Brunel they designed railways that cut through hills and bridged rivers. These were built by the railway navvies. Stations, signalling systems, railway tickets and fast travel all developed quickly after the first lines had been built.

Brunel also built steam ships that could travel around the world. Other engineers built steam cars and lorries but it was the railways that really made steam transport famous.

The cover of a magazine of the 1890s. It shows old and new forms of transport. ➤➤

Glossary

Act of Parliament An Act of Parliament is a law.

Cauldron A cauldron is a large cooking pot.

Electric telegraph The electric telegraph was a way to send messages along wires.

Embankment An embankment is a bank of earth. It was built for a purpose.

Garb Garb means clothes.

Gauge Gauge is a measurement. The gauge of railway lines is the distance between the lines. There was a broad gauge and a narrow gauge.

Locomotive A locomotive is something that moves from place to place. A locomotive is the engine part of a train.

Navvies Navvies were the men who worked on building the railways. The word is short for navigators. Navigators or Navvies built the first canals.

Parliament Parliament is where politicians debate and laws are passed.

Pick A pick is a long thin tool used for cutting into earth or rock.

Shovel A shovel is a broad tool used for lifting up earth.

Signal A railway signal is a sign which tells a train driver to stop or go.

Tonne A new tonne (metric) is 1000 kilograms or 0.984 old tons.

Viaduct A viaduct is a bridge carrying a road or railway over a valley.

Further information

Places to visit

National Railway Museum, York
Open: Monday to Saturday 10.00 a.m.–6.00 p.m.

Greater Manchester Museum of Science and Industry
The museum is set in the oldest railway station in the world.
Open: 10.00 a.m.–5.00 p.m. every day.

Darlington Railway Centre
School parties free, but you must book in advance.
Open: 9.30 a.m.–5.00 p.m.

Further reading

Train, Dorling Kindersley 1992.
(Look at its contents list to find out about Victorian trains).

Steam Trains by Bill Hayes, 1981, Albany Books.

Victorian Inventions by Leonard de Vries, 1991, John Murray.
(Available at Past Times).

Index

a b c d e f g h i j k l m n o p q r s t u v w x y z
A B C D E F G H I J K L M N O P Q R S T U V W X Y Z